MONSTERS

Witches

by Jennifer M. Besel

Reading Consultant:
Barbara J. Fox
Reading Specialist
North Carolina State University

Content Consultant:
David D. Gilmore
Professor of Anthropology
Stony Brook University
State University of New York

Capstone
press

Mankato, Minnesota

Blazers is published by Capstone Press,
151 Good Counsel Drive, P.O. Box 669, Mankato, Minnesota 56002.
www.capstonepress.com

Library of Congress Cataloging-in-Publication Data
Besel, Jennifer M.
    Witches / by Jennifer M. Besel.
    p. cm.—(Blazers. Monsters)
    Summary: "Describes the history and myths of witches, their features, and
their place in popular culture"—Provided by publisher.
    Includes bibliographical references and index.
    ISBN-13: 978-0-7368-6445-9 (hardcover)
    ISBN-10: 0-7368-6445-8 (hardcover)
1. Witches—Juvenile literature. I. Title. II. Series.
BF1566.B47 2007
133.4'3—dc22
                                                         2005037066

Editorial Credits

Aaron Sautter, editor; Juliette Peters, designer; Kelly Garvin, photo researcher/photo editor

Photo Credits

Art Resource, NY/Scala, 15
Capstone Press/Karon Dubke, cover, 4–5, 6, 8–9
Corbis/Bettmann, 23, 27; Underwood & Underwood, 26
Getty Images Inc./David Livingston, 29; Photographer's Choice/
    David Young-Wolff, 18; Taxi/Paul & Lindamarie Ambrose, 20–21
The Granger Collection, New York, 22
Mary Evans Picture Library, 11
Shutterstock/Winthrop Brookhouse, 19
SuperStock Inc./kwame Zikomo, 17; Superstock, 12, 25

Capstone Press thanks Tom Brooks and the staff of Meadowbrook Stables
in Mankato, Minnesota, for their help in making this book.

The author dedicates this book to her son Lucas, whose energy and love of
life are a magic potion all their own.

Table of Contents

A Midnight Stroll

While on a midnight stroll, a young woman sees an eerie glow. A raspy voice comes out of the darkness.

"Snakes, toads, and witch's brew," says the voice with a cackle. The woman creeps slowly toward the sound. Finally, she sees who is chanting.

It's a wicked witch! She's brewing a magic potion. The woman runs away before the witch spots her.

People with Power

Stories about wicked witches have been told for hundreds of years. Witches are not real. But many years ago, people thought they were.

Long ago, some men and women used plants to cure illness. Others thought these people had strange powers. Stories were made up about them, and they were called witches.

Many stories said that witches worked for the devil. The devil gave them power to cast spells. In return, they did evil tasks for him.

People once thought the devil looked like a beast with large horns.

15

Witch stories changed over time. Long ago, stories mostly described witches as old, ugly women. Wicked witches in newer stories have green skin and giant warts.

BLAZER FACT

Some stories said witches had "witch's marks" on their bodies. The marks could be birthmarks, moles, or patches of dry skin.

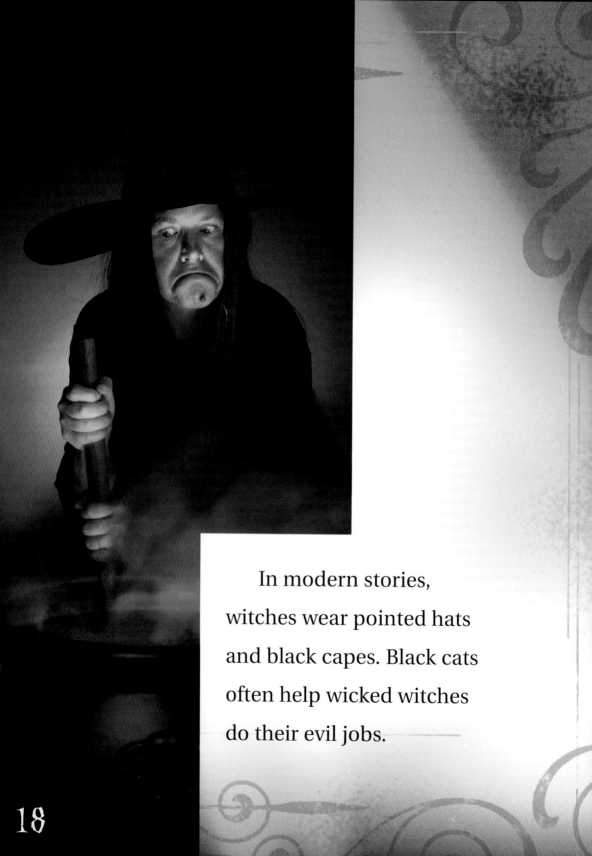

In modern stories, witches wear pointed hats and black capes. Black cats often help wicked witches do their evil jobs.

BLAZER FACT

Some people still think
they will have bad luck
if a black cat crosses
their path.

Stories say that witches can fly, change shape, and do other amazing things. Riding on a broomstick is a witch's favorite way to travel.

BLAZER FACT

Some witches can turn into animals or birds. They can go anywhere they want without being seen.

People once believed witch
stories were true. Long ago, people
hunted and killed men and women
they thought were witches.

BLAZER FACT

In 1692, more than 20 suspected witches were killed during the Salem Witch Trials.

Finding Witches Today

Today, children's stories are full of witches. Ugly, mean witches try to hurt good people. But evil witches never win.

In *Hansel and Gretel*, two children are trapped by a witch who wants to eat them.

Witches are also fun to watch in the movies. Wicked witches use their evil magic to cause trouble. Good witches like to help people.

In *The Wizard of Oz,* Glinda, the good witch of the North, helps Dorothy get home.

Witch costumes are popular on Halloween. Green faces and warts make you look scary. But that's the fun part of dressing up like a witch!

Glossary

chant (CHANT)—to say or sing a phrase over and over

eerie (EER-ee)—strange and frightening

evil (EE-vuhl)—wicked or cruel

popular (POP-yuh-lur)—liked or enjoyed by many people

potion (POH-shun)—a mixture of liquids thought to have magical effects

spell (SPEL)—a word or words supposed to have magical powers

MONSTERS

Read More

Crewe, Sabrina, and Michael V. Uschan. *The Salem Witch Trials*. Events that Shaped America. Milwaukee: Gareth Stevens, 2005.

Hamilton, John. *Wizards and Witches.* Fantasy and Folklore. Edina, Minn.: Abdo, 2005.

Martin, Michael. *The Salem Witch Trials.* Graphic Library. Mankato, Minn.: Capstone Press, 2005.

Internet Sites

FactHound offers a safe, fun way to find Internet sites related to this book. All of the sites on FactHound have been researched by our staff.

Here's how:

1. Visit *www.facthound.com*

2. Choose your grade level.

3. Type in this book ID **0736864458** for age-appropriate sites. You may also browse subjects by clicking on letters, or by clicking on pictures and words.

4. Click on the **Fetch It** button.

FactHound will fetch the best sites for you!

Index